Original title:
Past the Shadows

Copyright © 2024 Swan Charm
All rights reserved.

Author: Kaido Väinamäe
ISBN HARDBACK: 978-9916-89-790-4
ISBN PAPERBACK: 978-9916-89-791-1
ISBN EBOOK: 978-9916-89-792-8

Threads of the Celestial Loom

In shadows deep where whispers sing,
The sacred threads of love take wing.
In the hearts of those who seek,
The bonds of faith, both strong and weak.

The loom of life weaves destinies,
In harmony with cosmic seas.
Each strand a prayer, each knot a vow,
Binding us to the here and now.

Stars above, they shine with grace,
Illuminating this blessed space.
We gather hope in every stitch,
As we traverse life's holy pitch.

In trials fierce, we find our way,
Through darkest night to brightest day.
With every struggle, spirits grow,
The threads of love, they mend and flow.

So weave we now, with hearts aligned,
In unity, our souls entwined.
The celestial loom, our guide so true,
Threads of faith, forever anew.

Hymn of the Faded Light

In shadows deep, the whispers sigh,
The faded light, a gentle cry.
We gather round, in hope we stand,
Holding each other, hand in hand.

The echoes of grace, they softly fade,
Yet in our hearts, their power stayed.
With every prayer, a spark ignites,
To guide our souls through endless nights.

The flame may wane, but do not fear,
For love abides, and draws us near.
In times of doubt, let faith unite,
To cherish still the faded light.

The Resurrection of Forgotten Paths

In ancient woods where silence weeps,
A path once lost, the spirit keeps.
Awakened now by gentle breeze,
Reviving dreams from sleep's disease.

With each step taken, grace unfolds,
Through secret trails and stories told.
The flowers bloom where memories lay,
In sacred soil, they find their way.

From ashes rise the hopes we bear,
In shadows deep, we find our prayer.
The light returns, and hearts will sing,
To find the joy that love can bring.

The Silent Prayer of the Past

In quiet corners of the night,
The past unfurls, a soft, dim light.
With every sigh that breaks the still,
A silent prayer, a whispered will.

For voices lost, we yearn to hear,
Their timeless wisdom, ever near.
The stories woven in our veins,
Echoing through our joys and pains.

In moments fleeting, life's embrace,
We seek the comfort of their grace.
With grateful hearts, we turn the page,
In silent prayer, we share their stage.

Beneath the Eternal Canopy

Beneath the stars, in night's embrace,
We gather close, in sacred space.
The heavens gleam with tales of old,
In whispers soft, the truth unfold.

Each flickering light, a guiding star,
Reminds us we are never far.
From celestial realms, the blessings flow,
To light our paths, where blessings grow.

In unity, the hearts align,
Under the sky, our spirits shine.
Together bound, with faith we soar,
Beneath this canopy, forevermore.

Threads of the Celestial Loom

In the tapestry of night,
Stars weave whispers of grace.
Each thread, a flickering light,
Guiding souls in their place.

With every dawn that breaks,
Hope rises on the breeze.
Heaven's chorus awakes,
Singing peace among trees.

The loom of fate spins slow,
Casting shadows of prayer.
In the heart, love will grow,
Cradled in dreams we share.

Beneath the fabric's arc,
Divine hands gently sew.
Through the light and the dark,
In unity, we flow.

Embrace the sacred weave,
Trust in the paths we take.
In every heart, believe,
A promise that won't break.

The Lament of Haywire Winds

Winds howl through barren trees,
Echoing lost cries of yore.
They carry tales of unease,
Of hearts that dream no more.

Among the fallen leaves,
Memories twist and twine.
Songs of sorrow it weaves,
In the shadows, we pine.

Nature's breath, wild and free,
Calls to the weary soul.
In the tempest, we see,
Fragments of the whole.

Yet every gust that roams,
Brings change to weary ground.
From the depth of our homes,
New hopes shall be found.

In the silence, we raise,
Our voices to the skies.
For life's a fleeting maze,
Yet love never dies.

When Souls Whisper their Secrets

In the quiet of the night,
Souls exchange their hidden fears.
Softly, like stars shining bright,
Whispers blend, falling tears.

Beneath the moon's soft gaze,
Truths are shared without blame.
In the timeless embrace,
Hearts ignite the same flame.

Every secret held tight,
Finds a blessing in release.
In the shadows, hearts light,
Binding souls with sweet peace.

With every breath we take,
Promises linger like dew.
In trust, connections awake,
Threads of life, tried and true.

Thus, we gather and weave,
A tapestry strong and bare.
In the night, we believe,
Love is our greatest prayer.

Church of the Unremembered

In the ruins of lost time,
Echoes of laughter remain.
Silent prayers, sacred rhyme,
In this place, joy and pain.

The altar holds memories,
Faded scents of incense sweet.
In its heart, all that sees,
Every soul finds its beat.

Crenellations of dark days,
Whisper stories of the past.
Yet in sorrow's tangled maze,
Hope's light shines ever vast.

Gathered here in stillness,
Voices murmur, hearts unite.
In this hallowed witness,
Love transforms the darkest night.

For in this church of dreams,
Unremembered life can bloom.
Each shadow softly gleams,
In the grace of the room.

Beneath the Celestial Veil

Beneath the stars, a light so bright,
Guides weary souls through the night.
In shadows deep, His grace does flow,
A promise kept, where spirits grow.

He walks with those who seek His face,
In every tear, He leaves a trace.
With whispers soft, He calms the storm,
In faith's embrace, our hearts transform.

A path adorned with golden grace,
Through trials faced, we find our place.
A gentle hand in times of strife,
He gives us strength, He gives us life.

In holy light, our fears dissolve,
With every prayer, our hearts revolve.
United hope, like rivers wide,
In love's embrace, we shall abide.

Beneath the veil, our souls take flight,
In harmony, our spirits bright.
For those who seek, the truth is near,
In faith we find, no room for fear.

Echoes of the Divine Whisper

In silent prayer, we bow our heads,
To hear the voice where peace embeds.
A tender word, a gentle nudge,
In every heart, His love won't budge.

Through valleys low, through mountains high,
He bids us trust, and not to sigh.
For in the dark, His light will gleam,
Awakened souls will know His dream.

With every breath, His presence near,
Echoes of love, dispelling fear.
We rise as one, in unity,
In whispered truths, we find the key.

A sacred bond, a timeless call,
In every heart, He loves us all.
To walk with grace, to live in peace,
With every step, our doubts will cease.

In every soul, a spark divine,
With open hearts, His light will shine.
Together bound, we find our way,
In echoes soft, we choose to stay.

The Pilgrim's Reverie

A pilgrim's heart, in search of truth,
Through winding paths of vibrant youth.
In every step, a lesson found,
In sacred whispers, love unbound.

With hope afire, we wander wide,
In every moment, He is our guide.
Beneath the sky, our spirits soar,
The world unfolds, we seek for more.

In dusty trails, we leave our fears,
With every trial, He wipes the tears.
A compass set by faith so sure,
The way to peace, forever pure.

In unity, we lift our song,
A chorus sweet, both brave and strong.
The journey spans through time and space,
In love embraced, we'll find our place.

So onward now, with hearts made bold,
Through valleys low and mountains cold.
The pilgrimage, a sacred quest,
In Him we find our truest rest.

Radiance Beyond the Gloom

In darkest night, the stars will gleam,
A promise whispered in the dream.
Through hidden trails of hope we roam,
In faith's embrace, we find our home.

Each shadow speaks of love profound,
In every heartbeat, grace is found.
A radiant glow that lights the way,
In every dawn, the breaking day.

With every sorrow, joy will rise,
In depths of doubt, to see the skies.
He walks beside, our guiding flame,
To shine in darkness, glory's name.

In every path, a chance to see,
The beauty found in unity.
In shared belief, our spirits bloom,
With His embrace, we banish gloom.

The light of love, a beacon bright,
In every heart, igniting light.
For in our souls, His truth will reign,
A radiance pure, breaking the chain.

In the Embrace of Reverie

In quiet halls where silence dwells,
The whispers of the heart do swell.
In prayer's soft glow the spirit bends,
In reverie, where true love mends.

With faith as light, we walk the night,
In shadows deep, we seek His sight.
Each breath a hymn, each sigh a prayer,
In sacred bonds, we find Him there.

Through trials faced and burdens borne,
Our weary souls are softly worn.
Yet in His arms, we find our peace,
In love's embrace, our fears release.

The stars above sing praises clear,
As hope's sweet song draws ever near.
In unity, our voices raise,
To celebrate His endless grace.

So let us wander, hand in hand,
Upon this blessed, promised land.
In reverie's warm, eternal glow,
We find the path, we yearn to know.

Pathway to the Eternal Flame

On this path where shadows part,
A flicker lights the seeking heart.
Through trials faced and roads unknown,
The sacred truth is softly shown.

With each step forward, let us see,
The light that guides, the way to be.
Through thorns that pierce and winds that sway,
Faith leads us on, come what may.

The flame within, forever bright,
Illuminates our darkest night.
A guiding beacon, warm and still,
Awakens dreams, inspires will.

In moments fraught with doubt and fear,
The flame's sweet whisper draws us near.
Together, bound, we'll face the storm,
In love and light, we find our form.

As days unfold, we know our place,
In every heart, His holy grace.
The pathway forged, our spirits rise,
To the eternal flame, our cries.

The Spirit of Yesteryears

In winds that carry tales of old,
The whispers of the wise unfold.
In sacred texts, their voices dwell,
The spirit of yesteryears we tell.

Each lesson learned, a step we take,
Through trials faced, the hearts may break.
Yet in the past, our strength remains,
In memories, our hope sustains.

With open hearts, we seek the light,
From ancient stories, new insights.
The spirit guides us, hand in hand,
A journey shared across the land.

In quiet moments, we reflect,
On paths once walked, the lives we connect.
In gratitude, our voices raise,
To honor love in timeless ways.

So let us cherish every year,
And hold the wisdom ever dear.
For in the past, the future grows,
The spirit lives, and love bestows.

Flight of the Redeemed

Upon the wings of grace we soar,
In freedom found, we seek no more.
The chains that bound have crumbled soft,
In flight of faith, we rise aloft.

With every heart, a story shared,
Through trials faced, through battles dared.
In unity, our spirits blend,
The journey's end, the message penned.

Through valleys low and mountains wide,
We find the strength that's deep inside.
In joy and tears, we ebb and flow,
The call of love, forever grow.

In sacred circles, we unite,
To celebrate our shared delight.
The flight of the redeemed, we sing,
Of hope restored, of new beginnings.

So let us lift our voices high,
In harmony, we touch the sky.
With hearts set free, we dare to dream,
In flight of grace, we find our theme.

The Dust of Saints

In fields where saints once tread,
The whispers of their prayers still spread.
Soft echoes of a holy peace,
In sacred dust, our souls release.

Their footsteps linger, faint yet near,
Guiding us through doubt and fear.
With every breath, their love ignites,
A beacon bright on darkest nights.

Beneath the stars, we find our way,
In every dawn, their light holds sway.
Trusting in the path they paved,
In the warmth of grace, we are saved.

Though shadows come and tempests rage,
Their legacy is our sacred page.
In humble hearts, their story stays,
A testament through countless days.

So let us walk with faith anew,
In every dream, their spirit true.
For in the dust where they have lain,
The dust of saints will heal our pain.

In Search of the Lost Light

Through ancient woods and whispering trees,
We seek the light that sets us free.
Each shadow speaks of memory's song,
In search of the lost, we journey long.

The dawn advances, hope in hand,
With every step, we understand.
What once was bright is veiled from sight,
Yet faith remains our guiding light.

In silent prayers, our hearts ignite,
As stars awaken in the night.
The path ahead is fraught with care,
But grace will lead us, ever fair.

Through trials deep and valleys wide,
In every tear, our spirits glide.
For in the darkness, still we find,
The lost light kindles hearts aligned.

So let us shine amidst the gloom,
Where love transcends all fear and doom.
In search of light, we rise, we stand,
Together bound, as promised planned.

Embers of Afterlight

The night is cold, yet embers glow,
In whispered prayers, our spirits flow.
From ashes born, a flame takes flight,
Guiding us through the endless night.

In every heart, a spark remains,
A flicker bright amidst the pains.
Though shadows dance, they cannot claim,
The fire fed by love's pure name.

With open hands, we share the blaze,
Igniting hope through tangled maze.
In unity, our song adorns,
The embers glow as new day dawns.

From depth of darkness, light will rise,
Transforming hearts, clearing the skies.
For in each soul, the dusk will yield,
To embers bright, our faith revealed.

So come together, side by side,
In afterlight, our spirits guide.
With every breath, love's flame renew,
As embers warm, our purpose true.

Veils of Forgotten Grace

In silence draped, the veils unfold,
A tapestry of stories told.
Beneath the layers, truth abounds,
In forgotten grace, redemption grounds.

Each thread a prayer spun in time,
Echoes of love, a sacred rhyme.
Through trials faced, and joys embraced,
We find our strength in grace misplaced.

The past, a river flowing strong,
Carries the notes of ancient song.
In every tear, a lesson borne,
A promise kept, a light reborn.

So let us lift what's steeped in night,
Reveal the treasures, share the light.
For in the veils, our souls entwined,
The grace of love we seek to find.

Together forged through every phase,
In unity, embrace the maze.
Veils of forgotten grace, we trace,
To find the path that leads to grace.

The Choir of Silent Prayers

In the stillness, hearts unite,
Whispers rise into the night.
Each soul's longing, softly bared,
Together, we are gently spared.

Angels listen through the gloom,
Caressing sorrows, banishing doom.
Voices blend in sacred space,
Finding solace, love, and grace.

Every tear that falls in trust,
Lifts our cries, igniting dust.
In the silence, faith prevails,
Through our struggles, love unveils.

Hope ascends on wings of prayer,
In the echoes, we declare.
Singing forth our quiet plea,
A sacred bond, you and me.

In the choir of silent prayers,
God resides in all our cares.
With each breath, a promise stays,
In the night, we find our ways.

Lament of the Wandering Spirit

Beyond the valley, shadows creep,
A weary soul, no rest, no sleep.
Searching for a place to land,
Grasping fate with trembling hand.

Mountains speak of tales long past,
Each echo carries doubts amassed.
In the wilderness, I roam,
Yet yearn for a sweet home.

Night falls heavy on my brow,
With every step, I wonder how.
Questions linger, silence shrouds,
Amidst the dark, uncertainty crowds.

Oh, guiding light, where can you be?
In this tempest, set me free.
Let the soft winds show the way,
To peace, to love, come what may.

A lament sung to the stars,
Hearts alight with unseen scars.
For in wandering, I might find,
The spirit's truth, pure and kind.

Wisdom in the Wake of Shadows

In the twilight's gentle veil,
Wisdom whispers, soft as sail.
Shadows dance on echoes past,
Lessons learned, forever cast.

What once was, now fades away,
In the lessons of the day.
Through the sorrow, joy is spun,
In the dark, a light begun.

Every heart that loves, that grieves,
Holds the truth that hope believes.
In the quiet, answers grow,
From the shadows, truth shall flow.

Seek the comfort in the night,
For in darkness, there is light.
Each soul's journey finds its peace,
In the wake, we are released.

Gathered wisdom, softly sown,
In the heart, we are not alone.
Rise with grace, embrace the dawn,
For in shadows, dreams are drawn.

Celestial Fragments Gathered

Stars descend in graceful flight,
Gathered fragments of pure light.
In the universe's embrace,
We find hope in every trace.

Glimmers of a distant past,
Whispers of a love steadfast.
In the cosmos, dreams ignite,
Casting shadows, sparking bright.

Every moment, fleeting, rare,
In our hearts, the truth laid bare.
From the heavens, we discern,
Life's great lessons, ever turn.

As we gaze upon the skies,
Finding wisdom, free of lies.
Celestial fragments guide our way,
In the night, we long to stay.

Together, let our spirits soar,
In this dance, forevermore.
Fragments shining, never dim,
In the light, our hopes begin.

Light Reclaimed from Despair

In shadows deep, a faint glow shines,
Hope flickers bright, like distant signs.
From broken hearts, we rise anew,
With faith as our guide, we'll see it through.

In trials faced, our spirits mend,
Through whispered prayers, our souls ascend.
An ember's warmth in winter's night,
Together we stand, reclaimed in light.

Each tear we shed, a seed of grace,
In darkest times, we find our place.
With gentle hands, we take the chance,
Awakening love, a sacred dance.

As dawn breaks forth, despair will fade,
In unity, our strength is laid.
The burdens lifted, shadows clear,
In faith and trust, we cast out fear.

A beacon bright, through pain, we roam,
In every heart, we build our home.
With each embrace, the world we share,
Together as one, in love we dare.

Tresses of Time and Truth

In the weft of time, our stories spin,
Whispers of truth, where life begins.
Each moment held, a strand so pure,
In sacred space, our hearts endure.

The tapestry woven, each thread its role,
In luminous grace, we find our soul.
With every breath, the past and now,
We honor the journey, and humbly bow.

Through valleys low, and peaks so high,
In every tear, a reason why.
The stories told, from long ago,
In ancient light, our spirits glow.

With hands held tight, we rise in trust,
In faded dreams, we gather dust.
Yet every dawn, a chance to see,
The fibers of love that set us free.

As tresses flow, like rivers wide,
In unity, we choose to bide.
With every heartbeat, in truth we find,
The sacred bonds that intertwine.

Remnants of a Holy Light

In quiet nights, the stars take flight,
A promise kept, in sacred sight.
From ancient days, to futures bright,
Remnants linger, a holy light.

In whispered hymns, we find our peace,
From burdens deep, our woes decrease.
With open hearts, we seek the grace,
In every shadow, love leaves a trace.

Through trials faced, we shine anew,
In every soul, the flame breaks through.
The echoes of faith, a timeless call,
In holy whispers, we rise above all.

As candles flicker, in tabernacles vast,
The past entwined, with shadows cast.
Yet here we stand, in courage dressed,
In remnants of love, we are blessed.

So gather near, let spirits soar,
In unity, forevermore.
With every breath, the light will stay,
Guiding our hearts, come what may.

Pathways to Sainted Dreams

Upon the hill, where silence reigns,
We seek the path, where love remains.
With humble hearts, we tread the way,
In reverence deep, we choose to pray.

The stars align, each step divine,
Through valleys low, the light will shine.
In every heartbeat, a sacred song,
Together we journey, where we belong.

In every dream, the visions bloom,
In faith we walk, dispelling gloom.
With grace as guide, we seek the night,
On pathways paved in hope and light.

Through trials faced, we rise anew,
In unity strong, we find the true.
With arms outstretched, we claim our fate,
In sainted dreams, we navigate.

As dawn breaks forth, our spirits soar,
Together as one, forevermore.
In every moment, love's gentle beam,
Guiding our souls, on sacred dreams.

The Light that Beckons Back

In the quiet twilight glow,
A whisper calls from high,
Through shadows deep and low,
The light begins to sigh.

With each step I take,
The path unfolds anew,
Guided by the break,
Of dawn's soft golden hue.

In hopes that swell like tides,
I reach for what is true,
Where sacred love abides,
And grace will pull me through.

Oh, beacon shining bright,
Your warmth, a gentle balm,
In chaos, find my sight,
Restore my weary calm.

Let faith become my guide,
Through trials I must face,
In this, my heart confides,
To find eternal grace.

Elysium's Embrace

In fields where spirits dance,
Beneath a sky of dreams,
Heaven's sweet romance,
With radiant light it gleams.

The breath of angels sings,
In harmony they soar,
Upon their mighty wings,
They open heaven's door.

With every sacred tear,
The earth is blessed anew,
In joy, we cast our fears,
For love will see us through.

Elysium's gentle sway,
Wraps us in purest grace,
In the arms of the day,
We find our rightful place.

With every heartbeat shared,
Our souls joyfully meld,
In this love, we're ensnared,
A truth forever held.

Ciphers of Holy Memory

In silence, truths unfold,
In whispers of the heart,
Each story is retold,
In the past's sacred art.

The moments etched in time,
Like stars upon the sea,
A rhythm, pure and prime,
Our shared eternity.

Through trials long endured,
A tapestry we weave,
In faith, our souls assured,
That love will not deceive.

Within these ciphers bright,
We find divine design,
As shadows kiss the light,
In every soul, a sign.

Together we ascend,
In unity we stand,
With prayers, our hearts mend,
Awake to love's command.

Prayers Weave the Night

As evening blankets calm,
My spirit seeks the divine,
With every whispered psalm,
I dance in sacred line.

The moon, a gentle guide,
Illuminates my way,
In shadows I confide,
As night begins to sway.

With hands raised to the sky,
I weave my hopes and fears,
In silence, hear the cry,
Transforming pain to tears.

Among the stars that shine,
My heart reclines in grace,
In prayer, I find my sign,
A love I can't replace.

As dawn absorbs the night,
With faith, my spirit takes,
In every breath, a light,
A promise that awakes.

Ascending Through the Remnants

In the shadows of past grace,
We lift our hearts in solemn praise.
Each step tread on sacred ground,
Whispers of the lost resound.

From ashes, hope begins to glow,
In stillness, the wisdom flows.
Heaven's light breaks through the dark,
Guiding souls with gentle spark.

Upon the heights, we search for peace,
In trials, faith does not cease.
With every climb, our spirits soar,
To touch the heavens, evermore.

The remnants speak a truth divine,
In every heart, a sacred sign.
Together we journey, hand in hand,
Through the relics of this land.

Embrace the echoes, brave and bold,
For in their whispers, secrets told.
We rise above the scars we bear,
In unity, our souls lay bare.

In the Arms of the Echoing Silence

In quiet rooms where shadows breathe,
The sacred stillness, we perceive.
In silence, faith finds its wings,
And through the dark, the spirit sings.

A gentle touch upon the soul,
In absence, we become whole.
Around us, a celestial choir,
In every heartbeat, love's desire.

Through the void, a whisper calls,
In the barren, the spirit sprawls.
Here, in stillness, visions bloom,
Turning silence into room.

In the arms of calm, we lay,
Lost in the grace of yesterday.
Transcending time, we find our way,
Through echoing silence, we pray.

Held by the unseen, pure and right,
A beacon shines in the night.
In every pause, a truth revealed,
In silence deep, our wounds are healed.

A Pilgrimage to the Unseen

We set our feet on distant trails,
Where faith abides and love prevails.
With every step, a prayer we weave,
In search of truths that we believe.

Through valleys low and mountains high,
Underneath the vast, blue sky.
Guided by whispers of the heart,
Towards the journey, we impart.

In shadows cast by ancient trees,
We find the light within the leaves.
Each moment lived, a lesson learned,
In every corner, the spirit burned.

Across the waters, sacred streams,
Flowing gently as life redeems.
We seek the beauty, ever near,
In unseen realms, where love is clear.

A pilgrimage towards the light,
With open hearts, we take flight.
Together in this sacred roam,
In unity, we find our home.

The Oasis of Holy Reminiscence

In desert sands, memories lie,
Beneath the sun, the spirits fly.
An oasis springs from the heart,
Where timeless tales and dreams impart.

In tranquil pools of sacred thought,
The lessons of the past are sought.
Each ripple stirs the depths of grace,
In every drop, a holy trace.

The echoes of the ages ring,
Revealing truths that time can bring.
In quiet moments, we discern,
A glimmer of what we must yearn.

This refuge of the ancient wise,
A sanctuary to realize.
In reminiscence, we are free,
Embracing all that's meant to be.

To wander here is to be whole,
In the embrace of the wandering soul.
The oasis flows in harmony,
A place where hearts can truly see.

Glimmers of Promise

In shadows deep, hope dwells near,
A whisper soft, a gentle cheer.
The dawn will break, the night will flee,
With faith as light, we journey free.

In trials faced, our spirits rise,
Like birds in flight, beyond the skies.
A promise kept, in hearts we find,
The strength of love, the ties that bind.

Through valleys low, we find our way,
Each step a prayer, come what may.
In silence, grace begins to glow,
With every breath, we learn to grow.

For every tear that falls in vain,
A seed of joy will bloom again.
In unity, our voices chime,
Resilient hearts, transcending time.

Together we'll walk, hand in hand,
In sacred trust, a promised land.
The glimmers shine, they pave the road,
In faith we journey, love bestowed.

The Altar of Yesterday's Dreams

At dawn's first light, we gather round,
An altar built on sacred ground.
With whispered hopes, and silent screams,
We lay to rest our past's lost dreams.

In shadows thick, regrets unfold,
Yet heartbeats echo, brave and bold.
We lift our voices, soft yet clear,
In stories told, we persevere.

With every prayer, the burdens light,
A path revealed, a guiding light.
We share the weight of times long gone,
And find the strength to carry on.

Each memory sweet, a lesson learned,
In every corner, love's fire burned.
The altar stands, a timeless space,
Where dreams arise, and hearts embrace.

In unity, we stand as one,
The past embraced, the future spun.
Together we rise, from what's been hard,
The altar shines as hope's reward.

From Darkness, Grace is Born

In the stillness of the night,
A flicker glows, a whispered light.
From depths unknown, grace breaks through,
A tender spark, a chance anew.

In hearts once filled with doubt and fear,
The gentle voice of love draws near.
With every step, through pain we wade,
In shadows cast, our faith displayed.

From brokenness, a beauty grows,
In shattered dreams, new courage flows.
For every loss, a seed is sown,
From darkness springs the light we've known.

With every tear, a promise made,
In every scar, the price we've paid.
Together bound, in love we soar,
From darkness deep, grace is restored.

In gratitude, we find our place,
Embracing life with newfound grace.
From pain's great depth, our spirits rise,
In all of us, the light defies.

Light's Embrace on Worn Souls

In weary days, when burdens weigh,
The light breaks forth, it leads the way.
With every breath, a gentle sigh,
In light's embrace, the weary cry.

Through trials faced and shadows cast,
We find our strength in love steadfast.
With open arms, we welcome grace,
In tender moments, we find our place.

With light that warms the coldest night,
Our souls entwined in pure delight.
For every heart that's worn and torn,
In light's embrace, a hope reborn.

Together we rise, a chorus strong,
In harmony, we find where we belong.
The light will guide through darkest days,
Forever cherished, in endless praise.

In unity, our spirits thrive,
With every heartbeat, we come alive.
For light will lead us evermore,
In worn souls' journey, love will soar.

Beneath the Cloak of Time

Within the shadowed folds we dwell,
Each moment whispers, a sacred spell.
A tapestry of faith, woven tight,
Guided by stars in the depths of night.

The sands of ages slip like dreams,
Carried forth on celestial streams.
We search for truth in the vast unknown,
Beneath the cloak, we are not alone.

Hearts entwined in silent prayer,
Echoes rise in the evening air.
Silent mentors from ages past,
Their wisdom cradles our spirits fast.

In every heartbeat, a promise sounds,
In every stillness, grace abounds.
Through trials faced, our courage blooms,
Under the cloak, the spirit looms.

When shadows stretch and doubts arise,
We look for comfort in the skies.
For time is but a fleeting state,
In faith, we find a love that's great.

Veils of Divine Memory

Behind the veil, where whispers blend,
Echoes of angels, our hearts they mend.
Memory dances in light divine,
Restoring souls, as stars align.

In the stillness, secrets flow,
Stories of grace we long to know.
The pages turn, each lesson learned,
In sacred whispers, the heart is churned.

Fleeting shadows of what once was,
Moments etched in a cosmic cause.
With every breath, we draw them near,
The veils of time, delicate and clear.

As faith ignites, the past we weave,
Harvesting love in what we believe.
In the garden of memory, truth we see,
A tapestry rooted in divinity.

Through tears we've sown, and laughter gleaned,
Life's woven paths, forever dreamed.
In divine memory, we find our place,
Guided by light, in eternal grace.

Revelation in the Haze

In the mist where shadows play,
Clarity beckons, lighting the way.
A fog of questions begins to clear,
Revelations whispered, loud and near.

Beneath the clouds, the truth alive,
In every soul, the spirit thrives.
Guided by faith, we rise above,
In the haze, we find our love.

Moments merge, the past and now,
Each heartbeat's promise, a sacred vow.
The unseen hand that paints our fate,
In revelation, we cultivate.

When doubts arise like shadows tall,
We witness grace through the veils that fall.
For in the haze, a light will bloom,
A guiding flame that chases gloom.

With open hearts, we dare to seek,
In every struggle, we find the meek.
Revelation ignites the soul's embrace,
As we uncover life's holy place.

The Light Beyond the Eclipse

When darkness falls, we hold our breath,
For light will rise beyond its death.
The moon may shield the sun's warm glow,
Yet through the veil, the radiance flows.

In every trial, a heart reborn,
Through pain and struggle, hope is worn.
The eclipse, a moment, brief and bold,
A lesson wrapped in mysteries untold.

We gaze in wonder at the night,
In shadows deep, we seek the light.
For in the journey, shadows fade,
In faith's embrace, our fears are laid.

Waves of grace wash over scars,
Healing whispers carried by the stars.
Through every gap where darkness spun,
We rise again, united as one.

Emerging strong, the dawn is near,
With every heartbeat, we draw near.
To light beyond the eclipse we chase,
In unity, we find our place.

Ribbons of Faith Unfurled

In fields where whispers meet the sky,
Mighty spirits soar, they never die.
With every prayer, a ribbon glows,
Faith unfurled, as the river flows.

In shadows cast by doubt and dread,
Hope ignites in hearts once led.
Each step a promise, each breath a hymn,
Ribbons of faith, our spirits swim.

Through trials faced and storms endured,
A loving hand, our souls assured.
We gather strength from those who soared,
Mending hearts, our lives adored.

With each dawn's light, our voices sing,
In harmony, the peace they bring.
Bound by grace, the journey known,
Ribbons of faith, we're never alone.

United in love, we walk this road,
Guided by whispers, our sacred code.
Together we rise, in light we dwell,
In ribbons of faith, we weave our spell.

Celestial Pathways

Upon the hill where stars ignite,
Celestial pathways glow so bright.
With every step, the heavens call,
A dance of light, where shadows fall.

In silence deep, a truth unfolds,
Through cosmic threads, our fate beholds.
A tapestry of love, divine,
We journey forth, through space and time.

With open hearts, we seek the grace,
Embracing joy in every place.
In stardust dreams, our hopes align,
Celestial pathways, forever shine.

As comets blaze, the night's embrace,
We find our way, in sacred space.
Each blessing shared, a journey made,
In love's own light, we are remade.

So reach for stars, let spirits guide,
In harmony, be not afraid.
The universe sings, our souls unfurl,
On celestial pathways, blessings swirl.

Beyond the Veil of Fading Light

Beyond the veil, where shadows meet,
In quiet grace, our souls retreat.
A whisper's way, a sacred trust,
In fading light, we turn to dust.

Yet in the dusk, a spark remains,
Through tranquil dreams, the spirit gains.
In moments shared, love's essence glows,
Beyond the veil, the heart still knows.

In whispered prayers, our hopes ascend,
To realms unknown, where time can bend.
Each flicker of light, a journey's clue,
Beyond the veil, we start anew.

With every heartbeat, cosmic ties,
Unseen connections, where wisdom lies.
In fading light, our souls entwine,
Beyond the veil, in love we shine.

As we traverse the paths of night,
Seek the dawn, embrace the light.
For in our hearts, the truth is bright,
Beyond the veil, we take our flight.

A Journey to the Sacred Echo

Upon the hill where echoes dwell,
A journey calls, with stories to tell.
In every note, a memory rings,
A sacred echo, through time it sings.

With open hearts, we seek the sound,
In whispers soft, our souls are bound.
Through endless valleys, love will flow,
A journey deep, to the sacred echo.

In twilight's grace, where shadows play,
We find our path, choose love's own way.
In harmony, the world we mend,
A journey true, with heavens to blend.

The echoes guide, through night and day,
A sacred song, our spirits sway.
With every step, we draw so near,
To sacred echoes, we hold dear.

In unity, we lift our voice,
In love profound, we rejoice.
For in this journey, hearts will grow,
To find the truth, in sacred echo.

Cathedral of the Unseen

In shadows deep where silence reigns,
The whispered prayers lift like chains.
Within these walls, pure faith resides,
A sanctuary where hope abides.

Each echo speaks to souls long lost,
In the embrace of holy frost.
Beneath the arch of sacred light,
We gather hope in endless night.

With hearts aligned to heaven's tune,
Beneath the watchful, silver moon.
The unseen ties that bind us strong,
In this cathedral, we belong.

The flickering candles softly glow,
As currents of the spirit flow.
Here grief is cradled, love restored,
Within this space, we're all adored.

So come and seek the sacred peace,
In silence find your soul's release.
In shadows deep where silence thrives,
The cathedral's heart forever lives.

The Holy Quiescence

In stillness wrapped, where hope is found,
A gentle hush, a sacred sound.
The world outside fades far away,
In holy quiescence, we shall stay.

Soft whispers drift like autumn leaves,
In silence, truth the spirit heaves.
With every breath, we draw the grace,
Of tranquil faith in this embrace.

The sunlit rays through stained glass gleam,
As hearts align in peace's dream.
In quietude, our souls unite,
In holy quiescence, pure delight.

Here burdens lift and fears dissolve,
In stillness, every heart evolves.
With faith we tread on pathways bright,
In this embrace, we find the light.

So linger here, let troubles cease,
In gentle pause, discover peace.
In stillness wrapped, where hope is found,
Love's melody, forever crowned.

Hallowed Ground of Yesterday

Upon this soil, the echoes stand,
Of whispered prayers and loving hands.
Each stone a tale of ancient grace,
Hallowed ground, a sacred place.

The shadows dance with memories bright,
In the embrace of morning light.
Where faith was forged through trials lost,
In hallowed ground, we heed the cost.

Here generations buried deep,
In sacred slumber, silently sleep.
With every step, we honor they,
On hallowed ground of yesterday.

In every breeze, a soft refrain,
Reminds us of our joy and pain.
With every heartbeat, love endures,
In this communion, spirits soar.

So gather here, let time reveal,
The strength of hearts that learned to heal.
Upon this soil, the echoes stand,
In hallowed ground, we take our stand.

Starlight Over Stumbling Stones

When darkness wraps the world in dread,
And heavy hearts feel cold and dead.
Look up, for starlight breaks the gloom,
A beacon bright, dispelling doom.

Each shimmering light a guide through night,
Reminding us to seek the light.
In time of struggle, doubts that bleed,
Starlight offers hope, our hearts to feed.

Over each path, though rough and torn,
A glimmer shines, new joy reborn.
Through trembling steps on stones we tread,
Starlight weaves dreams, light the thread.

In every soul, a spark resides,
Through trials faced, the spirit guides.
With faith we walk, though shadows lean,
Starlight over paths unseen.

So when you stumble, dwell no more,
For starlit visions softly soar.
In darkest hours, trust the unknown,
With starlight's grace, you're never alone.

Threads of Light in the Dark

In shadows deep, a whisper glows,
A tender thread where wisdom flows.
Hearts entwined with hope's embrace,
In darkest night, we seek His grace.

Each star a voice, a prayer in flight,
Guiding souls through endless night.
With faith we tread on paths unknown,
In every tear, His love is shown.

When fears arise, and spirits quail,
His light will break through every veil.
A tapestry of love we weave,
In every moment, we believe.

So let us gather, hand in hand,
Together in this sacred land.
With every heart that dares to dream,
We find our strength within His beam.

Threads of light, forever bright,
Illuminate our journey's flight.
Through trials faced, we find our part,
In every thread, His guiding heart.

The Resurrection of Longing

From hollow graves of shattered dreams,
Emerges hope like sunlit beams.
A silent voice begins to sing,
In every heart, new life takes wing.

We wander through the paths of pain,
Yet in our sorrow, love's refrain.
Each longing, deep as oceans wide,
In His embrace, we safely glide.

The seasons change, the soul reborn,
From darkest nights, new days are sworn.
We feel the pulse of life anew,
In every breath, He comes in view.

So let us rise, like morning light,
Transform the dusk into the bright.
With faith that stirs each waking hour,
Our spirits bloom like summer's flower.

In every longing, we find grace,
The Resurrection, our sacred space.
With every heartbeat, we proclaim,
In love's revival, we'll rise again.

Beneath the Gaze of Eternity

In quiet moments, time stands still,
A sacred breath, an unwritten will.
Beneath the gaze that sees us whole,
We find the light that fills the soul.

The universe, a canvas wide,
With stars that dance, with waves that ride.
In every glance of sacred sky,
Our spirits soar, our hopes comply.

In prayerful whispers, hearts align,
With every pulse, our thoughts divine.
Together bound by love's decree,
In every echo, we are free.

Each moment holds His gentle trace,
In every tear, we see His face.
With faith as firm as mountains stand,
We walk the path, hand in hand.

Beneath the gaze that knows our plight,
We find our peace in purest light.
In every heartbeat, He remains,
In love's embrace, the soul regains.

Harbingers of Solace

In quietude, where spirits weep,
Harbingers of solace sweep.
With gentle hands, they mend the fray,
And guide the lost along the way.

From ashes rise the seeds of hope,
As broken hearts learn how to cope.
Each whispered prayer, a soft caress,
In every wound, we find the bless.

In storms of doubt, they stand as light,
With courage born from darkest night.
Through trials faced, our spirits grow,
In every shadow, love will show.

So gather, seekers, near and far,
Embrace the light, each guiding star.
In every heart, a song will swell,
The harbingers that weave our shell.

Through all of time, their voices blend,
In every love, they find their end.
With solace in each heart's refrain,
Our spirits rise, like gentle rain.

Drifting Through the Veil of Ages

Across the river of time I roam,
Guided by whispers from the unseen dome.
Each moment a lesson, a page unturned,
In the heart of the cosmos, I sought and learned.

Stars sprinkle wisdom on night's dark canvas,
With each passing hour, a divine purpose.
In the silence, I find the sacred call,
Through love and forgiveness, I rise from the fall.

The echoes of prayers linger in the air,
Stories of faith wrapped in celestial care.
I trace the footsteps of the ancients' way,
In the light of their grace, I find my stay.

Drifting on currents of mercy and grace,
I gather the truth in this sacred space.
In the depths of my soul, the light shall reign,
As I wander through ages, free from all pain.

Beyond the horizon, new realms await,
With each blessed moment, I resonate.
Embracing the journey, through shadows and light,
In the fabric of time, my spirit takes flight.

A Tapestry of Sacred Memories

Threads of gold weave through my mind's eye,
Moments of grace that never say goodbye.
With each stitch a prayer, a love divine,
In the quilt of existence, our souls entwine.

The laughter of children, a melody bright,
Stories of old that warm the night.
In the glow of candles, the past resonates,
As I honor the love that patiently waits.

Holding the hands of those who've passed,
In dreams they whisper, their spirits steadfast.
Together we travel, across the wide sea,
In the sacred tapestry, they live in me.

Woven with hope, every color and thread,
The fabric of faith that never is shed.
In ceremonies humble, we gather in peace,
In joy and remembrance, our sorrow will cease.

With love as the needle, stitching our fate,
In every heartbeat, I cherish and wait.
For the thread of existence binds us in grace,
In the tapestry of memories, we find our place.

Shadows of the Divine Journey

In the quiet of twilight, I seek the divine,
Where shadows dance softly, and spirits align.
Every step whispers the tales of the past,
In the echo of footsteps, our truths are amassed.

The moon paints a path on the waters below,
Illuminating journeys where hearts ever glow.
Each flicker of starlight reveals hidden ways,
Guiding the pilgrims through nights and through days.

Among the lost realms, the saints softly tread,
In shadows of love, where angels have led.
Carving our stories in the fabric of night,
In the depth of our longing, we find sacred light.

The horizon unravels, mystery unfolds,
Whispers of wisdom wrapped in pure gold.
Every moment a treasure, lovingly stored,
In the heart of the journey, we're endlessly soared.

Through valleys of darkness, and peaks of pure grace,
We carry each other in this sacred space.
In shadows of the divine, we gather and weave,
In the journey of faith, we forever believe.

The Sacred Repository of Time

Hidden within silence, the treasures reside,
A repository rich with love as our guide.
Moments like diamonds, they shimmer and shine,
Each heartbeat a promise, divine and benign.

Memories linger like sweet, fragrant blooms,
Whispering secrets in twilight's soft glooms.
In the shelter of grace, we find our way home,
In the arms of the past, we never alone.

Every tear that has fallen, a river of grace,
Carved in the landscapes that time can't erase.
Through the passage of years, wisdom does flow,
In the repository sacred, love's essence will grow.

With hands intertwined, we embrace all the years,
In the fabric of moments, we weave out our fears.
Finding strength in the stories, we share and we tell,
In the sacred repository, forever we dwell.

As dawn paints the heavens with hues of the day,
We carry the light, come what may.
In the sacred, we trust, through the rise and the fall,
In the repository of time, we find love through all.

Seraphic Dreams of Ancients

In the quiet night, angels weave,
Whispers of wisdom, hearts believe.
Stars align with a golden thread,
Guiding the lost, the weary, the dead.

Echoes of prayers rise soft and free,
Through timeless realms, they dance with glee.
Faithful shadows in the pale moon's glow,
Bathe us in dreams from long ago.

Wings unfurl as spirits inspire,
Carrying hope, igniting the fire.
In silence, we seek the truth so vast,
To cradle the moments, holding the past.

Celestial beams light the ancient ground,
In sacred rings, our souls are found.
Let every heartbeat echo His name,
In this seraphic dream we proclaim.

Unity formed in ethereal grace,
Together we rise, in love's embrace.
With every breath, we rise and we fall,
Seraphic dreams unite us all.

Illuminations in the Gloom

In shadows deep where silence dwells,
Faith ignites like distant bells.
Hope unfurls in the darkest night,
Painting our hearts with sacred light.

With every tear a story unfolds,
Of love and loss, the brave and bold.
Underneath burdens, grace shines through,
Illuminations whispering, 'I am with you.'

The path ahead may twist and bend,
Yet in the gloom, we find a friend.
His presence steady, like a flame,
Guiding our hearts, calling our name.

In trials faced, our spirits soar,
Reverberations of faith, evermore.
When darkness looms, together we stand,
Illuminations forged by His hand.

In the quiet dusk, where shadows creep,
Dreams are sewn, and souls are deep.
Through every storm, we shall persist,
In gloom's embrace, love will assist.

The Altar of Resilience

Upon the altar, resilience grows,
Burnished stones where the heart bestows.
Each trial waxed into a prayer,
Forged in the fires of sorrow and care.

Hands uplifted, we break our chains,
In tears and laughter, love remains.
Strength derived from the struggles faced,
At the altar, hope is embraced.

Whispers of valor echo the halls,
Courage built where love enthralls.
Through every challenge, we rise and mend,
The spirit shines, a faithful friend.

On this sacred ground, we find our worth,
Rooted in faith, in joy, in earth.
With every heartbeat, we stand anew,
At the altar of resilience, pure and true.

Together we sing in unison bright,
Overcoming shadows, seeking the light.
For in each struggle, we craft our song,
At the altar of resilience, we belong.

Grace Under the Surface

In waters deep where secrets lie,
Grace flows softly, like a sigh.
Beneath the surface, wisdom waits,
To calm the storms, and open gates.

Hearts unburdened, gentle and wise,
The silent prayers, the soft replies.
Every ripple an echo of grace,
Guiding souls to a warmer place.

The depths of spirit, rich and profound,
In stillness, we hear the holy sound.
Though trials may come and shadows cast,
Through grace, we rise, steadfast and vast.

Each moment cherished, a drop of light,
Journeying forth, we ignite the night.
In the quiet depths, we find our worth,
Grace under the surface, a rebirth.

Together we flow, a river of dreams,
Unified hearts in love's gentle beams.
In every current, His touch we trace,
Embracing the beauty of grace.

Transfigured by the Light

In shadows deep, the soul takes flight,
Awakened by the soft, pure light.
A whisper calls from realms above,
Embracing all with boundless love.

With every step on sacred ground,
In silent awe, the heart is found.
Transfigured by this golden grace,
In gentle peace, we find our place.

The light reveals what's lost and true,
Each broken piece restored anew.
In harmony, we dance and sing,
United by the flame of spring.

Through trials faced and tears we weep,
In faith's embrace, our souls do leap.
The light of hope within us glows,
In darkest nights, a promise flows.

We walk in faith, our burdens light,
Each step a prayer, each breath a rite.
Transfigured by the radiant beam,
In the Father's love, we dream.

Celestial Bridges Forged

Upon the skies, where angels soar,
We build the bridges to the shore.
With hands intertwined, we reach above,
Connecting souls through boundless love.

In every heart, a light takes hold,
Courage blooms in the midst of gold.
We journey forth, with spirits bold,
Bearing witness to tales untold.

Each echo of a prayer ascends,
A symphony where each heart blends.
Together we rise, together we stand,
In sacred trust, where true hearts land.

The stars align, their messages clear,
For every doubt, God draws us near.
A tapestry of grace we weave,
In faith we trust, in grace believe.

As dawn ignites the sleeping night,
The world transformed by radiant light.
Celestial bridges, strong and bright,
Invite us home, unite our plight.

A Testament of the Lighted Path

In quiet moments, wisdom calls,
A testament to rise from falls.
The lighted path, though hard to see,
Reveals the truth that sets us free.

Through whispered prayer and open heart,
We journey forth, hand in hand, we start.
Each step we take, a sacred vow,
With faith as compass, here and now.

The burdens borne shall light transform,
In every storm, we find the warm.
Through every trial, love prevails,
In mystery, the spirit sails.

A candle lit in darkest night,
Illumines all with gentle light.
The guiding star, forever bright,
A testament of hope in sight.

With open eyes, we see the way,
In love's embrace, we freely sway.
A lighted path, a holy dance,
In every heart, a second chance.

When the Light Breaks Through

In silence deep, the shadows fall,
Yet whispers stir, a sacred call.
A promise blooms with morning's hue,
When every heart can feel it true.

The light breaks through, a tender grace,
Illuminating every place.
With love's embrace, our fears take flight,
In joy we rise, toward the light.

As dawn awakens weary souls,
The joyful song of grace extols.
In every tear and every laugh,
The light restores, an endless path.

When doubts arise and shadows loom,
We find our strength within the bloom.
In unity, we will not sway,
For in the light, we find the way.

When the light breaks through the veil,
Love's gentle touch will never fail.
In every heart, the fire ignites,
A world reborn in sacred sights.

The Arch of Forgotten Grace

In shadows deep, where whispers dwell,
A grace once known, we long to tell.
The arching heavens, a silent song,
Reminds our hearts where we belong.

Old paths we've walked, in faith we tread,
With every tear, our souls are fed.
The fragrance sweet of love divine,
Awakens hope in every line.

Through trials faced, in darkest night,
We find the strength to seek the light.
An echo calls from distant shores,
To mend our souls, to heal the sores.

Beneath the stars, we raise our prayer,
For every heart, for every care.
The arch of grace, forever stands,
Embracing all with open hands.

In unity, we find the way,
To live in truth, to rise and sway.
With every breath, our spirits rise,
In forgotten grace, we seek the skies.

Echoing the Sacred Silence

In sacred hush, where spirits soar,
The silence speaks, forevermore.
Within our hearts, a truth unbowed,
In quiet faith, we stand unclouded.

The whispered winds, a gentle breeze,
Carries our hopes like autumn leaves.
In tranquil moments, wisdom flows,
The sacred silence brightly glows.

Through binding chains of earthly fate,
We rise above, we contemplate.
In shadows cast, our souls ignite,
With every prayer, we seek the light.

In endless peace, our spirits dwell,
A tale of love, we weave and tell.
The echo calls, a sweet refrain,
In sacred silence, we remain.

So let us pause, and breathe the air,
In stillness found, we lay our care.
For in this space, where love aligns,
Echoing hearts, our faith defines.

The Footprints of Reverence

Along the path of sacred trust,
We leave our mark, in faith we must.
With every step, we honor grace,
Footprints left in this holy place.

In every gesture, kindness flows,
Reflections of the love that glows.
Through trials faced, our strength is born,
In reverence, we are reborn.

The journey wide, the distance vast,
Yet hand in hand, we hold steadfast.
With each heartbeat, a pledge we make,
To cherish love, for love's own sake.

In quiet moments, wisdom speaks,
A gentle guide for tired weeks.
The footprints of those who came before,
Inspire us all, forevermore.

So let us walk with hearts aligned,
In reverence for the ties that bind.
For in each step, a promise made,
The footprints left, a love displayed.

Fading Light, Rising Faith

When evening falls, and shadows creep,
In fading light, our fears we keep.
Yet in the dusk, a promise glows,
A rising faith in all we chose.

Each star that shines, a guiding ray,
In darkness deep, it lights the way.
Through trials faced and doubts embraced,
We find the strength our hearts have chased.

With every dawn, new hope appears,
To wash away our doubts and fears.
In every tear, a lesson learned,
Through loss and love, our spirits yearned.

In unity, we stand as one,
Through fading light, our battles won.
For in the night, our faith ignites,
A beacon bright, through endless flights.

So let us rise, as shadows fade,
In every breath, our fears cascade.
For in this journey, strong and free,
Fading light gives rise to thee.

The Pilgrimage of Seen and Unseen

In the valley where shadows dwell,
Hearts tread softly, secrets to tell.
Faith whispers sweet in the breeze,
Guiding souls with gentle ease.

Mountains loom, their peaks so high,
Echoes of prayers reach the sky.
Every step a sacred rite,
Walking hand in hand with light.

The road we follow is worn yet bright,
Carved by promise, shaped by night.
Each stone a story, each turn a grace,
Leading us to a holy place.

In silence, we seek what's divine,
In unison, our spirits entwine.
For unseen hands guide our way,
Through shadows that bend night to day.

With every breath, we find our peace,
A pilgrimage that'll never cease.
The seen and unseen, forever blend,
In the love that knows no end.

Clothed in Reverence

Wrapped in whispers, hearts unfold,
Clothed in reverence, like ancient gold.
Every thread a story sewn,
In sacred garments, truth is grown.

The fabric of faith, both strong and light,
Draping our souls in divine sight.
Embracing grace in every fold,
With love woven, and warmth untold.

Hands raised high, we offer prayer,
In humble moments, stripped of despair.
Covered in love, we stand as one,
Under the gaze of the eternal sun.

In silence, we breathe the sacred air,
Clothed in hope, beyond compare.
Each heartbeat echoes a solemn vow,
To honor the present, cherish the now.

With every dawn, we shine anew,
In sacred attire, pure and true.
For in this reverence, we unite,
Clothed in love, we embrace the light.

Lanterns of Olden Belief

Flickering softly in the night,
Lanterns glow with ancient light.
Each flame a prayer sent above,
Whispers of hope, whispers of love.

Through the dark, they guide our way,
Illuminating paths where shadows play.
With every spark, the past resides,
In stories told where faith abides.

These lanterns hold the dreams of old,
In their warmth, our hearts unfold.
As they dance upon the breeze,
They unveil truths with gentle ease.

In the stillness, we find our peace,
With faithful hearts, we're never ceased.
Each flicker a bond, a sacred keep,
In the glow of belief, our spirits leap.

So let us gather, hand in hand,
With lanterns bright, we take our stand.
For in their light, we're never alone,
In unity, our faith is grown.

Hymns of Embraced Remnants

In shadows deep where remnants lie,
We sing our hymns to the sky.
Each note a memory, soft and clear,
Embraced by love, we hold them dear.

With voices raised in harmony,
We weave our dreams into the sea.
Every echo tells a tale,
Of journeys marked, of hope's avail.

The remnants speak of trials past,
Each struggle builds a love that lasts.
With broken pieces, we create,
A tapestry of hope, our fate.

In joy and sorrow, we find our way,
Through hymns that lift, come what may.
For in these remnants, life anew,
Is found in every shade and hue.

So let us gather, hearts aglow,
In hymns of love, let our spirits flow.
For in embraced remnants, we rise,
With timeless beauty that never dies.

Songs of the Spirit's Lament

In shadows deep the spirit cries,
For lost moments beneath the skies.
With whispers soft of grace untold,
A tale of longing, a heart of gold.

In prayerful nights and mourning days,
We seek the light in winding ways.
Each tear a note, each sigh a plea,
For peace and hope, our souls set free.

O'er barren lands, where silence reigns,
The spirit wanders, bound by chains.
Yet in the dark, a flicker glows,
A promise kept, the heart still knows.

With hands uplifted, we implore,
To mend the bonds, to heal the sore.
In every hymn, our voices rise,
A sacred bond that never dies.

Remembered joys, the laughs we shared,
In sacred bonds, our spirits bared.
For every loss, a seed is sown,
In love's embrace, we're never alone.

The Vessel of Yesterday

In quiet corners of the past,
Where memories linger, shadows cast.
We find the echoes of our prayer,
In vessels worn, in tender care.

With gentle hands, we hold the dreams,
Of yesteryears, like flowing streams.
Each blessing poured, each tear released,
In love's embrace, our souls find peace.

These vessels hold both joy and pain,
In every storm, in every rain.
Yet through the trials, wisdom grows,
In heart's reflection, love still flows.

From ancient roots, our spirits rise,
With open hearts and searching eyes.
In every tale, the truth is spun,
Together bound, we are as one.

So lift the chalice, toast the night,
As weary souls are drawn to light.
For in the past, we find our way,
A vessel forged, in love's array.

Crowned in Ethereal Light

Beneath the stars, in tranquil grace,
We seek the dawn, a sacred place.
The spirit shines, a guiding ray,
As night surrenders to the day.

In every heart, the light will dance,
Awakening dreams, a holy chance.
With every breath, we rise anew,
In radiant love, forever true.

The crown of light, it glimmers bright,
A reminder of our sacred fight.
Through trials faced and battles won,
In unity, we find the one.

With hands entwined, we lift our gaze,
In harmony, our spirits blaze.
A chorus sung from depths untold,
In love's embrace, we are consoled.

So let your heart be filled with grace,
Crowned in the light, in love's embrace.
For in this realm, forever free,
We find our strength, our destiny.

Chronicles of Forgotten Grace

In whispers soft, the tales unfold,
Of grace once lost, and love retold.
Within our hearts, the stories lie,
A sacred bond that will not die.

With every heartbeat, we recall,
The moments cherished, shadows thrall.
In every smile, the grace shines through,
A tapestry of light anew.

We gather strength from days of old,
In every tale, the truth is bold.
Through storms we've passed, and trials faced,
We find the light, though time erased.

So let us sing of days gone by,
With hopeful hearts, we reach the sky.
In chronicles penned, our stories blend,
A legacy of love, without end.

And in the quiet, there is peace,
A promise made, our souls release.
With every breath, we live this grace,
In unity, our hearts embrace.

Journey Through the Halls of Time

In whispers soft, the echoes call,
Through corridors that never fall.
Each step a prayer, each breath a hymn,
Beneath the watchful gaze of Him.

Time bends and sways, a sacred dance,
In every trial, there lies a chance.
To find the light in shadowed days,
And walk with faith in His holy ways.

The past fades gently, like morning mist,
In every moment, His love exists.
We carry forward, with hearts made pure,
As we seek the truth, alone, unsure.

Through ancient worlds, our spirits roam,
In search of wisdom, we find our home.
The sands of time, they slip and glide,
Yet in His presence, we abide.

Each memory lingers, a sacred tie,
Bound by hope as the ages fly.
With open hearts, we tread this path,
Embracing the journey, the holy aftermath.

The Sanctum of Hidden Blessings

Within the stillness, treasures lie,
In whispered prayers, our spirits fly.
A tranquil heart reflects His grace,
In every moment, we find His face.

Beneath the veil, the secrets sleep,
In humble hearts that joyfully keep.
The gifts of love, so sweetly shared,
In quiet corners where souls are bared.

Each blessing counts, a star in night,
A guiding light, so pure and bright.
We gather strength from what we find,
In hidden paths, our souls entwined.

The sanctum built from faith and prayer,
Each cherished breath, a sacred layer.
With open hands, we search for grace,
In the still waters, we find our place.

With every tear, a bloom will rise,
In darkest times, the heart's surprise.
For in His love, abundance flows,
From hidden blessings, our spirit grows.

Reflections of Grace

In mirrors bright, grace softly gleams,
In every heart, a thousand dreams.
Reflections cast in light divine,
A treasure trove in every line.

With every trial, forgiveness blooms,
In the quiet, His love resumes.
We find redemption in every glance,
Embracing hope, we take our stance.

The paths we walk, both rough and clear,
Are marked by faith, dispelling fear.
Through valleys low and mountains high,
Our spirits soar, our souls rely.

In gentle moments, grace unfolds,
In stories shared, our truth beholds.
With hearts awakened, we sing His praise,
In life's reflections, His light displays.

Crafted in love, our journeys blend,
Each twist and turn, a trusted friend.
Through every shadow, grace weaves tight,
In our reflections, we find true light.

Wings of the Unseen

With wings of faith, we soar on high,
Where earthly bounds begin to die.
In whispers soft, the Spirit calls,
To rise and dance beyond the walls.

Each heart is lifted, each soul takes flight,
In shadowed moments, we seek the light.
The unseen wings that guide our way,
Through storms of night, toward break of day.

In every prayer, a gentle breeze,
That fills our sails with heartfelt ease.
We find our strength in sacred trust,
In love that binds, in faith that must.

The wings unfold, embracing grace,
In every trial, our sacred space.
With open hearts, we boldly rise,
Exploring realms beyond the skies.

So let us cherish this holy flight,
With wings of hope, we chase the light.
In every moment, let us see,
The unseen realms that set us free.

Embrace of the Ancients

In silence, echoes of old reside,
Wisdom flows like rivers wide.
Under stars, the stories weave,
In the night, the heart believes.

Beneath the branches, shadows dance,
In each heartbeat lies a chance.
A prayer whispered on the breeze,
Carried forth with gentle ease.

The earth remembers every prayer,
In the burden of our care.
Ancient spirits guide our way,
In the light of dawn's first ray.

With open arms, we seek the grace,
In every wrinkle, every face.
The joy of living, deeply sown,
In every heart, we are not alone.

Together, hand in hand we stand,
Embracing all, a sacred band.
The whispers of the past ignite,
A flame within, forever bright.

Whispered Secrets of the Hearth

Around the fire, shadows play,
In the warmth, we find our way.
Ancestors speak in crackling tones,
In their wisdom, we are known.

With every ember, stories rise,
Glimmers of truth beneath the skies.
Through every silence, love prevails,
In the heart, the spirit sails.

Gathered near, our voices blend,
In each refrain, the souls ascend.
Every whisper, a guiding star,
Illuminating who we are.

The strength of kin, a bond we share,
In trials deep, we show we care.
From hearth to heart, the light cascades,
Through whispered secrets, hope invades.

In laughter's glow, we find our peace,
In shared moments, love's increase.
The stories linger, never fade,
In the hearth, our prayers paraded.

The Eternal Flame of Remembrance

Within the stillness, memories blaze,
A flicker of love through the haze.
In the absence, their voices sing,
An eternal bond, a sacred ring.

Each candle lit, a prayer released,
In remembrance, the heart is eased.
Their laughter dances on the breeze,
In our hearts, they dwell with ease.

Through seasons passed, their light remains,
A guiding star through joys and pains.
In every moment, they are near,
In our hearts, we hold them dear.

With every sunset, we look above,
Finding comfort in their love.
The eternal flame, it flickers bright,
Illuminating the darkest night.

Together, we honor every tear,
In shared silence, we draw near.
In the whispers, their spirits play,
An endless love that guides the way.

Fragments of the Divine Tapestry

In threads of gold, the stories lie,
Woven close to the boundless sky.
Each colorful strand, a tale retold,
In the fabric of faith, we behold.

From the heavens, wisdom flows,
In every stitch, the spirit grows.
The tapestry of life unfolds,
In sacred patterns, love beholds.

Through trials faced, we find our grace,
In unity, we hold our place.
Each moment a piece of the whole,
In every heart, the divine soul.

In shared laughter, and whispered sighs,
We find the truth between the lies.
The divine plan, both vast and true,
In each heart, a spark anew.

Together we create, we mend,
In the tapestry, we ascend.
With joy our guide, we journey free,
In fragments whole, eternally.

Pathways of the Dusk

In whispers deep, the shadows play,
Guiding souls at close of day.
Upon the paths where silence dwells,
A sacred truth within us swells.

Each step we take, we leave a mark,
A light that flickers in the dark.
For in the dusk, the spirit glows,
And in its warmth, the heart then knows.

With every breath, we seek the light,
Through tangled branches, out of sight.
The light of faith, a beacon bright,
Unfolds our journey, pure and right.

The stars above begin to sing,
Of hope and grace each moment brings.
In twilight's arms, we pause and pray,
And trust the path will guide our way.

In harmony, the night will swell,
With stories old and tales to tell.
As dusk transforms, we stand in awe,
Embracing love, divine and raw.

Sacred Footsteps in Twilight

Upon the ground, beneath our feet,
Sacred pathways meet and greet.
In twilight's glow, we take our stand,
With open hearts and outstretched hands.

The echoes whisper of ancient lore,
In every step, we seek for more.
Touched by spirit, the night ignites,
A dance of faith in countless lights.

Each footfall soft, a prayer set free,
In sacred balance, you and me.
The stars above, our guiding song,
Binding us to where we belong.

As shadows weave a gentle thread,
We walk together, spirits bred.
Through twilight's hush, we find our way,
In love's embrace, we choose to stay.

With every breath, a promise made,
In unity, we won't be swayed.
In sacred steps, we find our truth,
Illuminate the path of youth.

In this twilight, we rise with grace,
Finding solace in our space.
Together we are strong and whole,
As sacred footsteps bless the soul.

The Dawn of Lost Hopes

In shadows cast, where dreams once soared,
We gather near, in hearts restored.
The dawn arrives, a soft embrace,
Reviving hopes in sacred space.

With every ray that kisses ground,
The whispers of lost dreams abound.
In fractured light, we seek to mend,
A promise held, on it depend.

Through trials faced and tempests fought,
We find the lessons life has taught.
With open hearts, we rise anew,
The dawn of possibilities grew.

With faith as guide, through shadows creep,
In stillness, we find strength to leap.
For every loss, a seed is sown,
In sacred ground, our roots have grown.

Each moment shared, we heal the past,
In unity, our love will last.
The dawn reminds us of our worth,
In every corner of the earth.

So let the light embrace our fears,
As hope ignites through countless tears.
In dawn's soft touch, we all are free,
To rise anew in harmony.

Essence of the Holy Echo

In quietude, we seek the sound,
The holy echo all around.
Whispers soft in sacred air,
Remind us of our answered prayer.

From heart to heart, the message flows,
In every beat of love that grows.
The echoes dance through time and space,
Uniting souls in warm embrace.

In gentle tones, the spirit calls,
Within the silence, beauty sprawls.
As night unfolds, the stars align,
Revealing truths that brightly shine.

Through trials faced and paths unknown,
The essence of love will be shown.
With every breath, the message clear,
In every echo, we draw near.

With faith as compass, we shall find,
The whispers of the divine kind.
In holy echoes, we belong,
Together in a faith-filled song.

So let us listen, hearts entwined,
For echoes flourish without time.
In sacred sound, we come alive,
The essence of love will always thrive.

Starlit Memories in Reverence

In the quiet night sky, stars shine bright,
Whispering stories of love and light.
Each twinkle a memory, a sacred dream,
In reverence we gather, a celestial theme.

Hearts lifted high, we bow our heads low,
For the grace of the heavens, we humbly bestow.
The echoes of ages, in silence they speak,
Guiding our spirits, as we seek.

Through the veil of the night, shadows of grace,
In starlit reflections, we find our place.
With whispers of hope, like a gentle embrace,
In unity we stand, in this sacred space.

Memories cascade, like a river of tears,
Washing away doubts, and all of our fears.
In the tapestry woven, each thread a link,
We find our purpose, in the moments we think.

So let us remember, as we gaze above,
The starlit memories, a testament of love.
In reverence we honor, the paths we've crossed,
In the heart of the cosmos, nothing is lost.

The Flame that Guides

Through shadows of despair, a light will arise,
A flame that ignites, beneath the vast skies.
In the depths of our souls, it flickers and glows,
A beacon of hope, in the darkness it flows.

With each sacred breath, we nurture the spark,
Illuminating the journey, through the night so dark.
In whispers of prayer, our spirits entwine,
Together we flourish, like the grape on the vine.

Along winding paths, where doubts often roam,
The flame shows the way, guiding us home.
In the dance of the fire, we find our true song,
A harmony vibrant, where we all belong.

As storms may encircle, and shadows may fall,
The flame that guides us, it conquers it all.
With courage and faith, we rise from the ash,
In the warmth of its glow, we find our path dash.

So honor the flame, for it burns within,
A reminder of light, where beginnings begin.
In the tapestry woven, by love's gentle hand,
The flame that guides us, forever will stand.

Devotion in Darkened Corners

In corners where shadows tend to reside,
Devotion shines through, a radiant guide.
No matter the darkness, love finds a way,
In whispers of faith, we are never astray.

With each secret prayer, a light we instill,
In the heart of silence, we bend to His will.
Through trials and pain, our devotion takes flight,
A fire unyielding, in the stillness of night.

We gather in spaces where few dare to tread,
Finding solace in words, where angels have led.
In unity forged, our spirits entwined,
In the depths of the corner, our hearts are aligned.

Through moments of doubt, when shadows loom large,
We cling to the light, and our spirits recharge.
For in the dark corners, true love is revealed,
In devotion's embrace, we are lovingly healed.

So let us remember, in shadows we find,
The grace of our love, eternally kind.
In darkened corners, where light ever glows,
Devotion unfolds, as the heart's canvas shows.

The Sacred Dance of the Past

In echoes of time, we sway to the beat,
A sacred dance, scripted by fate.
With each gentle step, memories alive,
In the rhythm of history, our souls derive.

From whispers of ancients, our spirits take flight,
In the warmth of their wisdom, we find our light.
Each movement a story, each turn a prayer,
Embracing the past, we breathe in the air.

With grace in our hearts, we honor the way,
The sacred dance calls, inviting to play.
In the tapestry woven by laughter and tears,
We celebrate growth, transcending our fears.

Through moments of silence, our souls intertwine,
In shared understanding, together we shine.
With each step in rhythm, we flourish and flow,
In the dance of the past, our love ever grows.

So let us not forget, as we move through this fast,
The sacred lessons learned, in the weave of the past.
In twilight's embrace, as we dance and we sing,
We honor the journey, the gifts it will bring.

Illuminated Remnants

In the shadow of the night,
Whispers of the angels soar.
Echoes of grace ignite,
Illuminating the core.

Each tear that falls like rain,
Cleanses the wearied soul.
In silence, peace we gain,
As faith makes us whole.

Through trials we ascend,
With courage by our side.
Hope whispers, 'It's not the end,'
In love we shall abide.

The remnants of lost days,
In dawn's light, we find anew.
With prayers and endless praise,
Our spirits are born anew.

Hearts like lanterns burn bright,
Guiding us through the fight.
In darkness, we seek the light,
With faith, we claim our right.

The Sanctity of Lost Time

Time flows like a gentle stream,
Carving paths through hearts of clay.
In each moment, hope's bright beam,
Guides the lost, showing the way.

We gather pieces of our past,
In the tapestry of grace.
Though shadows may loom steadfast,
In love, we find our place.

Every prayer a gentle breeze,
Whispers soft upon the air.
In stillness, we find our ease,
In memory, a sacred prayer.

Though days may drift and wane,
In the twilight of our days,
The sacred echoes remain,
A symphony of praise.

Let not the hours slip away,
Cherish each moment divine.
In faith, we embrace the play,
For in love, all things align.

Tides of Hope and Memory

The tides of time bring forth the past,
Waves crashing on the shores of fate.
In the stillness, shadows cast,
Hope and memory resonate.

Each heartbeat tells a story true,
A dance between the lost and found.
In faith, we rise like morning dew,
In quietude, grace does abound.

The ocean's song, a soothing balm,
Carries whispers of long-lost dreams.
In every wave, we find the calm,
Navigating life's winding streams.

As stars emerge in the night sky,
We gather light from days gone by.
In remembrance, our spirits fly,
With love, we learn to simply try.

Let every tide become a prayer,
Washing over us with care.
In hope, we lose the weight we bear,
Finding peace in memories rare.

Transcendence in the Twilight

As day yields to the night's embrace,
We wander through realms unseen.
In twilight's glow, we find our place,
A bridge between the in-between.

The whispers of the ancients call,
Carried on the evening breeze.
Within their echo, we stand tall,
In faith, our spirits find release.

Each star a promise, brightly shines,
Guiding weary souls along.
In the stillness, wisdom aligns,
In darkness, we uncover song.

Though shadows fall upon the land,
The heart knows not of despair.
In unity, we lift our hand,
In love, we find our prayer.

Transcendence flows through quiet night,
In moments where we feel the grace.
With every breath, we seek the light,
Together, we embrace the space.

Whispers from the Forgotten

In shadows deep, where silence sighs,
The echoes linger, age-old cries.
Lost hearts murmur, hope deferred,
In hushed repose, await His word.

The clouds above, they weep and mourn,
Yet in the gloom, new grace is born.
A flickered flame, a sacred spark,
Guides weary souls from night to hark.

The barren ground begins to bloom,
In whispered prayers, dispelling gloom.
The seeds of joy take root in sorrow,
Thy light, O Lord, shines bright tomorrow.

Through shadows cast, we seek Thy face,
Each tear a balm of love and grace.
In every whisper, the promise clings,
Of hope reborn and angel's wings.

With faith as guide, we rise and stand,
United in Thy holy hand.
Forever bound by sacred ties,
In whispered love, our spirit flies.

Light Beneath the Veil

In twilight's glow, where dreams take flight,
A subtle glow dispels the night.
Behind the veil, soft truths reside,
In gentle whispers, He'll abide.

The stars above in chorus sing,
Of sacred peace that faith can bring.
Our hearts aflame, we seek the light,
That shines through shadows, pure and bright.

Each step we take, a path divine,
Where love transcends and spirits shine.
In every trial, we find the way,
To reach the dawn of a new day.

The light that flickers in the dark,
Illuminates the smallest spark.
O faith, arise; let courage swell,
In every heartbeat, hear His spell.

Beneath the veil of doubt and fear,
The sacred whispers draw us near.
Embrace the grace that knows no end,
A light unhidden, a boundless friend.

Echoes of Celestial Grace

In harmony, the heavens call,
With echoes sweet that fill the hall.
Each note a prayer, each word a guide,
In celestial grace, we shall abide.

Beneath the stars, our spirits soar,
To realms of love forevermore.
The whispering winds, a gentle hand,
Will carry us to a promised land.

The beauty of the night unfolds,
In every tale of love retold.
The heartbeats sync with time's embrace,
A dance of souls in sacred space.

The echoes linger, forever free,
In every heart, a melody.
Let faith arise and softly sing,
Of hidden truths and angel's wings.

Through trials faced and burdens borne,
The echoes lead to hope reborn.
In celestial light, our spirits face,
All sorrow fades in His embrace.

The Sanctuary of Silent Souls

In quiet corners, spirits dwell,
The lost and broken seek to swell.
In silent prayers, their voices rise,
In sacred hush, where sorrow lies.

The sanctuary holds each yearning heart,
In gentle light, we'll never part.
Within these walls, love finds a place,
In every tear, a touch of grace.

The sun will shine after the rain,
In this holy space, no more pain.
With whispered hopes, we gather near,
To soothe the souls and calm their fear.

A refuge found in faith's embrace,
Restoration blooms in truth's sweet grace.
Each heart a story, each life a prayer,
In unity, we find Him there.

The silent souls now sing aloud,
In joy proclaimed, they wear their shroud.
With every breath, His love we find,
In the sanctuary, hearts aligned.

Through shadows cast, we stand as one,
Together basking in the sun.
In silent moments, grace unfolds,
The stories shared, the truth retold.

Milton Keynes UK
Ingram Content Group UK Ltd.
UKHW031320271124
451618UK00007B/194